ABOUT THE AUTHOR

Beth Calverley is a poet, performer, facilitator and founder of
The Poetry Machine.

Alongside her supportive Poetry Machine, Beth travels far-and-wide to
places of work, care, learning and play. She creates poems with people of
all ages, helping them to find words for their thoughts and feelings.

Beth is Poet in Residence at University Hospitals Bristol & Weston NHS
Foundation Trust and was published in *These Are The Hands*, the NHS
anthology. She has been a Poet in Residence for The Poetry House in
Ledbury (2021-22), a Bristol Poetry Festival Resident Poet (2021), a Bristol
Life Awards Arts Finalist (2020) and a Roundhouse Slam Finalist (2018).
She has worked with the BBC, ITV, Sky and many more.

Beth has performed at iconic venues such as Birmingham Hippodrome,
Bristol Old Vic and London Roundhouse. She also performs as part of
House of Figs, a music and poetry duo, and co-produces Milk Poetry, a
nurturing platform for spoken word in Bristol.

www.thepoetrymachine.live
Instagram: @poetrymachine
Twitter: @BethCalverley
Facebook: @ThePoetryMachineUK

The poems in the collection look at how smiles adapt to challenging times as well as positive ones. They explore experiences of mental ill-health (including trauma), physical ill-health, grief and loss. The book contains references to:

abuse
accident
alcoholism
anxiety
blood
bullying
childbirth
death
depression
divorce
eating disorder
hospitalisation
loneliness
loss of a loved one
memory loss
mental illness
pain
physical illness
PTSD/trauma
violence

20th May '22

Beth Calverley
Brave Faces & Other Smiles

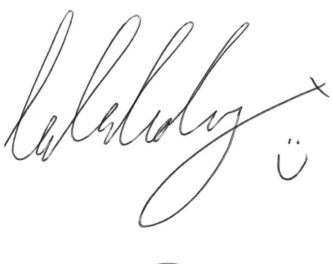

VERVE
POETRY PRESS
BIRMINGHAM

PUBLISHED BY VERVE POETRY PRESS
https://vervepoetrypress.com
mail@vervepoetrypress.com

FIRST PUBLISHED DEC 2020

Printed and bound in the UK
by ImprintDigital, Exeter

ISBN: 978-1-912565-40-5

Cover Design & Interior Illustrations by Kieran O'Shea

for all the smile-bringers

CONTENTS

Thankyous

FOREWORD

When I wrote *Spellbound*, the first poem in this collection, I noticed that smiles burrowed their way into most of my poems; perhaps because it took me a long time to feel confident in my own smile.

I investigated the science behind smiling, intrigued by its privileges and paradoxes. Studies show that people who smile are perceived as more trustworthy and competent. They even live longer. So, what happens when our smiles are pressurised? In human interactions, smiles can be windows into each other's worlds or doors swinging shut between us.

As a collaborative poet, I felt it was important to invite others to contribute their experiences of smiling, as well as my own. You'll notice that some of the poems have a dedication beneath them. '*With thanks to so-and-so*' means that the poem is inspired by a smile story that someone has chosen to contribute. '*For so-and-so*' means that the poem is unconsciously inspired by a close friend or family member and included with their blessing.

Even so, this collection does not attempt to cover every type of smile. There are many that don't feature (pun intended), including the fascinating cultural nuances of smiling. If you're interested in further exploration, I suggest starting with *Why Smile? The Science Behind Facial Expressions* by Marianne LaFrance and the references at the end of her book.

Thank you so much for picking up my collection of smiles. I hope they keep the rain at bay.

Take care,

Beth Calverley

NB - Many of the poems in the collection look at how smiles adapt to challenging times as well as positive ones. They explore experiences of mental ill-health, physical ill-health, grief, loss and trauma. See Page 3 for details.

Brave Faces
& Other Smiles

Spellbound

Amidst the silver clouds and spectacles,
I met you:

lady with the loveliest smile I've ever seen.
History rippled your cheekbone map from lip to ear,

cauldrons so clear
I knew straight up
you were magic.

Silence slurped at your cup,
a tiny trick that gave you substance.

Spellbound, I edged closer.

Back then, I was invisible;
too shy to smile without looking for the pieces
of pushed luck in my soul's reflection,
too shy to risk cracking my face in case it caved.

To me, your laughter lines were loud, sudden.
They drew me in.

The purr of your perfume,
the sheathed claw of your beauty
hinted at a life not read to girls at bedtime.

Your smile was the shock
of near-bad luck turned good.
A black cat walking the right way.
A magpie, joined in the end
by the flutter of a friend.

That's when you looked straight at me,
like a glass of cold water.

I spilled my thoughts in awe –
appalled at my own daring,
I told you

I really like your smile

and, to my surprise,
you gave it to me.

Wriggle

for Eva

'...*a real mouth-smile always has an eye-smile to go with it*'
– Roald Dahl, *Danny the Champion of the World*

Your room is a tangle
of buttery light.

I'm an honoured guest
in your teddy-packed bed.

Radiator-hot, you kick
the covers off.

There's time for one story – *one*.
Just twenty years older, I'm already

yawning; soon I'll be gone.
The title you show me

wriggles through my brain.
This was my favourite when I was your age.

When we reach the bit about smiling,
my voice is a delicate déjà vu.

Show me an eye-smile, you ask.
Now just your mouth.

You inspect my eyes each time,
the way you might check

my chin for yellow light
to tell if I like butter.

Satisfied, you nod,
to show you've learned

a truth I wish you
didn't need to know.

My arms tighten
around you, squeeze,

shrugged off like a cover.
Carry on reading please.

Eye Test

Growing up, I saw
trees as green clouds
drawn by young gods
learning to
keepbetweenthelines.
They told me to look

up

down

left   right

until my retinas wriggled
with flecks of light.

Out on the pavement,
where the sign read 'Eye Tests',
the ground had lines I'd
never
      known to
            side-step.

The world swept   forward
            for her encore.
I clapped her face
with my eyes.

All the names they'd
call me in the playground
blurred.
I glimpsed a textured life.

Each
separate
leaf   on   that   tree
across the road
was now
forever mine;

the world a pencil
– sharpened –
just for me
        to find.

Hindsight is a Playground Water Fountain

At the front of the queue,
a girl I try to avoid

has finished her drink.
She wipes her chin,

looks me up and down,
and calmly reports:

Your hair looks like a poo.

I've done it differently today,
spent ages preening

in the wishing well
and she can tell.

Her smile is a too-
tight scrunchy.

In years to come, at other water-fountains,
I'll remember every cleverness I never said.

Instead: *I know it does*, I shrug,
and, thanks to her, I really do.

Her scrunchy pings. *You know?
You want your hair to look like a poo?*

I turn my face away.
She tightens her smirk

and leaves the queue.

Early

for my life-giver

You made yourself a question I solved
with my body. An echo, born too soon.
Half a twinned miracle home from the womb.

We still joke that birth was the first
and only time in my life I wasn't late –
I couldn't wait to teethe what you cut for me.

So new that my fingernails were promises, my skin
thick with softness, crawling your belly
like the first monkey swung from mud.

And yet, at minus two months,
I wasn't early enough – no room at the ward for us.
They found us a cupboard, with no plug to feed me heat,

and fretted at my temperature (a daughter only by degrees).
You stripped bare, the answer to steady my question.
Skin against skin, I warmed to the world,

a borrowed belonging you dressed me in.
You taught me to answer life with questions
and hold on tight. On anxious days,

you dimmed the lights and we danced
together, grappled in a graceful fight,
shaking out the folds of flight.

Now I'm grown, I still forage in your wardrobe,
like Lucy, bound for Narnia, looking for home.
I find mine in your smile – each one a crumpled poem

and your voice – a hand on my forehead,
a lamp in my forest, back to our cupboard to dance
with the lights out, reaching into the furred darkness.

Sing-Along

That Christmas Eve, we drove for hours;
a tired theatre, a sleepy cast of four.
Miles of Joseph and his Technicolour Dreamcoat
later, we were going strong.

I'm not exactly proud of it but, as a girl,
I sang along to every colour in that coat –
even ochre, which I didn't *really* know.
The car, layered with blankets,

held us close; a musical of moving metal.
Mum and Dad took turns from wheel to map;
nothing extraordinary about that
but, this time, a row about directions –

stuck in the wrong lane.
Jazz-hand anger, door-slam drama,
a grown-up at the roadside in the rain.
Silent windscreen steamed with hurt.

Then the opened door, the making up,
the weight of hard, unscripted words.
I bickered with my brother in the back
until we drifted off on handy props.

When our legs were cramped as tempers,
it was time for a twist in the plot –
the longed-for petrol station stop.
In danced the technicolour air

to sweep our stuffiness away
and, finally, the tell-tale rustle;
our cue to ask what snacks
they'd got us in the break.

Usually, the rustle was the map
consulting with a parent's lap,
which led to disappointment in the back.
This time, they handed us

some *sorry* in a plastic bag
before the engine cleared its throat
to usher in the second act.
Of course, I wish my parents hadn't split,

but the colour ochre still exists
and colours never dreamed of can't be missed.
My cheek against the glass of any car
can take me back to it –

our cosy mess of seatbelts, love and limbs,
as blobs of brake-lights danced their exit,
trembling
like lips.

Measuring

for my not-so-little brother

We scaled the wall by the scruff of our
spines, learned to test the pressure of our
lives for a pulse – promise under papered
veins. We cast each other's shadow with a
pencil and tape; shoulders squared, chin
straight, to judge the length from sole to
brain. The day you were born, I stood on
tip-toes to take your measure, caught to her
breast on the hospital bed. Warm, un-
skimmed, like bedtime drink. Sip-sized, big-
eyed, a virgin nightcap. I asked when we
could play together; captain ships and pray
for treasure, polaroids and grainy weather.
The answer was ages, so I lost interest in
siblings – begged to put you back again. No
room in the world's slow womb for both of
us. Adventures came round soon enough;
wellies treading question-marks to feel our
puddles answering – bathtimes bubble-
barbering. Every green space beckoned a
race, each branch a sheathed lance. I honed
letting-you-win without you noticing. You
were with me when our childhood changed.
All faces and forearms, we rocked together,
cradled in coarse calm. We packed the past
in tissue-paper, still warm despite the line
drawn – a bath of storm clouds – eyes
cleaned like teeth before bed. These days,
you spill a shadow rich to paddle in; taller
every time you stretch at breakfast. Now,

your hugs have grown to fit *my* head under your lion-cub chin. In the race with no finish line except ceiling, my hare halts to take your tortoise in: that anti gravity of character, your cryptic wit a fickle fist we carry with us – packed punchlines – flock of seagulls in your grin. Now you're old enough, we visit gigs to sing our lullaby without a sound, cradled by the sibling love of crowds, the best of ourselves marked down: what's left, after all, when the rest is papered over. Tonight, your first mosh pit's friendly fire kindles you. I stop to watch your height take flight: shoulders squared, chin straight, feet strong, focusing.

Somehow, you've been winning all along without *me* noticing.

Jack-in-the-Box

With thanks to Sharlz

Some smiles are shy
and come alive in private.
Full of harmless tricks,

they crouch inside the box
until the trapdoor flips.
Only friends can find the hinge.

They press the magic x
that no-one else could guess –
and up comes the spring

with its bobbing grin:
the kind of smile
that lifts the sky a bit.

Lavender

'Why have you forsaken me?... I am poured out like
water, and all my bones are out of joint. My heart
has turned to wax; it has melted within me'. – Psalm 22

Her world has wound to a plot
of curtain. Nurses reel it round to keep
her secret safe. She closes her eyes
and imagines her garden at home.

Her partner pours the tea and calls to their son,
who sits on the mower, playing a captain.
She watches him riding the rapids, relieved to see
he's a boy, despite all the adult that's happened.

The nurses dissolve the curtain.
Her smile is a disinfected surface.
They leave her clean and freshly-dressed,
bees called from bed-to-bed.

She's always thought
that lavender is meant for pensioners.
It smells like old folks' homes. Now,
well-meaning people bring her droves

of scented candles, lavender of course.
Another one of life's cruel jokes.
One day, in a cloud of pain, she hits
a nurse with a glass jug.

Later, clear again,
she weeps, attacked
by the proof of his
lavender bruise.

When the chaplain comes,
she doesn't name her faith.
When she calls out in darkness,
only the staff answer.

A sign on the door describes
how she likes her tea. She's changed
her mind since she arrived, but they
bring it to her, sugared, every time.

The curtain closes again.
She shuts her eyes; imagines the garden.
Wax hardens, the moment passes,
and she's fine, she's fine, she's really fine.

She knows the change
will come from nowhere sudden –
only from her own slow
honeycomb of courage.

Now you see it, now it's...

with thanks to Mick

I know a gentle Cornish man
who slams his hand on the table
and vows that cream comes *after* jam.

He's fought worse battles than that,
although he leaves them out
and we don't ask.
The answers hide
in his laughter lines.

Once, his troop of paras landed by a lake,
stripped to uniform shivers,
and skinny-dipped
amongst the ice.

The warmth in his grin
when he talks of that swim
rekindles the comfort
he caught in the cold.

He takes a triumphant bite of scone,
embarks on another "good old time",
and leaves a mouthful of missions untold.

Decades after hanging up his boots, he got a call.

A member of his former troop
was lost
to the cubes
at the foot of his glass,

lured by the shivery music of ice,
dropped by the parachute past.

It's hard for me to understand
why gentle men like them
would go to war. I think
it has something to do
with the thought of
controlled falling,

that maybe we
can choose
where we
land.

Keeping Busy

When someone is sick,
we keep busy with random tasks.
Upstairs, despite it all, a laugh.
We wait by the window, aimlessly.
A grown-up points. *You see that tree?*
It's always been quick to bloom.
(The first sudden laugh in a quiet room.)
That's why it autumns early. Leaves ruin the grass.

We take the hint and fetch some rakes.
The air is a windfall apple to crunch.
Grown-ups watch us rake the lawn
where we played as children years ago.
A window's open – we catch that laugh,
gold raked over grass.

Activist

With thanks to Jackie

She used to have
a "Resting Bitch Face".

People teased her for it
or assumed she disapproved.

Now she lives with chronic pain,
she hardly lets her smile rest.

Some days, its fate is fixed,
her face a growl reclaiming *bitch*.

On other days, her smile is quick
to balance out the days she missed –
she waves it like an activist,
its protest singing from her lips.

Enter!

With thanks to Judy

Three middle-aged children sit by the bed
where their father rehearses his final breath.
They feel too formal, comically Victorian,
with odd bowed heads.

Each minute is a mournful wardrobe
holding back the black. Knock, knock,   knock.
A cheery wooden joke. News travels slowly
in the nursing home.

The carer doesn't know that, just inside,
an airborne wardrobe hinges wide.
For a moment, there's an awkward pause –
before their father, on his so-called death-bed,

bellows *ENTER* with propellant force,
his body powered upward by his voice,
a burst of everything he was – and is – in life.
Perhaps there's still a bit more time

for humour –
this unexpected heirloom,
bringing back
the light.

The Problem with Solving

'Loneliness is solitude with a problem' –
Maggie Nelson, *Bluets*

Dad's favourite story is the time
I downloaded his entire music library by accident.

It overwrote everything
and all my teenage tunes,
lovingly ripped from YouTube,
were lost to Joni Mitchell's *Blue*.

At first, I felt pure pain.
I thought the gods of taste had turned against me.
Then, like blood into stone,
Joni's lyrics trickled home.

I coloured-in her songs of solitude
and learned how Dad felt when Mum left.

The world had a crossword clue
even *he* couldn't solve,
his life a Cryptic forever unticked,
his smile a grid he fretted to fill...

but I watched him dance at a second wedding
where his eyes were a blazing cliché.
Now, when I listen to *Blue*,
I feel a lighter shade of calm

because the final note won't last
and the only mistake to make

is regretting the past.

Baddies

1951

She was a girl when baddies
were seen and not heard.

Disaster tipped from ships to streets,
her father's visits bittersweet,
bottled by his pockets,
pigeon-hole fists stuffed like sockets.

No specialists to cork his "madness"
for the forties were a story
read from ration books,
tight beyond their time.

When she was a girl,
baddies were second-hand shoes,
stares that pinched and pity in pigtails.
Her mother fed them cobbled courage.
Bellies, empty on bad days,
rumbled hope on good ones.

Somehow she raised her sister
on strength's legacy, left when
love that birthed them stopped.
They were fostered by scorn
in homes that hit back
every time their hearts beat.

1969

Her magic turned Smash into anything – even "meat pie!"
She served her empty-cupboard spells
to hungry daughters, when her husband,
raised on legends of a better ending,
left her reading stories she never rationed at bedtime.

Years later, when those daughters
'fessed to seeing therapists,
her eyes were clenched fists,
a girl again, hiding from baddies.

2012

Her third deserter
kept his word to cancer
over wedding vows.

This husband didn't mean to leave –
but he was gone.

A hand beside her in the cinema.
Favourite replays on a faded screen.

With him, she'd been young,
in new shoes, off to see the pictures.

At the funeral, she found notes stuffed in sockets,
uncorked at the coffin – death
of rationing – spilling *all* of it.

Epilogue

After that, she tasted therapy –
better than she's ever been,
despite his empty seat,
his pronoun kissing
every sentence of her life.

When she was a girl,
baddies lived in cupboards,
under beds – not in heads.
Now they live in ration-books again.

When will help become a balm
that's granted while we're hurting;
not just once we've suffered
long enough to earn it?

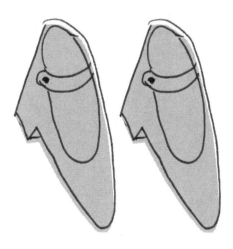

Who is it for?

'Wearing a face that she keeps in a jar by the door.' –
The Beatles, *Eleanor Rigby*

Keys still singing in the dish,
she opens the lid
to drop it in –

a sigh of relief
as she pops the kettle on for nettle tea.
At half past three, she fetches it

to watch the local kids go by,
wrapped in a dream by the window,
wearing her brightest *I'm fine*.

Their parents call her lonely –
they mouth the word, a soundless slur.
She sees its smear in their glances,

like wiping their hands of dirt.
Keep your "lonely" hidden to the grave;
bury its curse along with my name.

On the way to bed,
she pauses
by the door

for one last spin
before the mirror in the hall.
I'll show you who it's for.

I'll Hide, You Seek

Developed with Bethany M. Roberts

Arrival

One month, I found you in the house.
I looked downstairs
and there you were:

a streak of scarlet tomboy,
running free, always messy-haired.
You left your presence everywhere –

white pants, bare legs, cream chairs.
We learned to play a ritual of games.
I hid behind my hands, trickled down the days,

and came across your hiding place.
Once, I wasn't in the mood to play
so, when you closed your eyes to count,

I shut myself away –
waited in the wardrobe
while you called my name.

You peeked your face round
every door. I felt a thrill of guilt
and hid a little more.

At first you called me
through your smiles,
then with soft impatience,

then with quiet loneliness.
I stopped myself from shouting out,
strangely terrified to guess your name.

Soon it was time to end the game.
My silence underlined your loss.
Your disappointment dried in drops.

Departure

You took your crimson anorak
and left, our future bundled in your arms,
your face a blue-moon smudge of past.

When you left me like a sigh,
I felt completely fine. Calm.
I tidied up. The chores were done.

My room was clean. I settled down
to look for peace. The corners
of our former quarters

hosted games of cat and mouse
where only I was playing now.
Make-believe had taken over me.

I counted down to nothing
and went to look
for nobody.

Homecoming

Months skipped by like siblings, holding hands.
I drifted round the garden, touching fruit
from pips we'd placed in pots

before I ever knew the taste of loss.
I let my palms get messy –
juice as sweet and red as yours.

My apples gave themselves away
like smothered giggles
in a game of hide and seek;

a friendly note to help myself
beside a surplus pile of weeks.
At last, I felt your knock

at my threshold of a throat.
I struggled not to swallow you
and welcomed softness home.

In time, we learned to play again;
we chased each other, day and night,
to try our playroom out for size,

counting days like children
down to Christmas.
Finally, I found you:

a blossoming wish,
a songful of sin,
my prodigal gift,

waiting like sleep
in the wrapping
of my sheets.

Teatimes

'Suddenly there was a ring at the door' – Judith
Kerr, *The Tiger Who Came To Tea*

1.

Tiger,
you came to tea,
delivered in a doorbell
that filled our forks with pause.

Mummy got the door.
You dodged her legs, a confident guest
I scooped to my chest like a promise.

Mummy was worried.
She'd heard of tigers eating homes,
whole, from households –

but she was a fresh track back from hospital,
hunted by hurt,
legs preyed upon by shakes,
weak-winged healing,
tumble of bird.

So, Tiger, we fed you.

At teatimes, you sipped from my saucer,
ate from my plate, craving a taste.
Pink licked milk from fingers
grateful to trade
for a friend, at last,
to tame school's wildness;

a purr I packed under jumpers,
muffled from eyes,
lunch never lonely
with you by my side.

In bartered bites, your lies enlarged
to fill our mirror.
You gobbled the girl in the glass,
starved of pride by pilfered dinners.
Patterns we'd grown for stealth
grew hard to hide.

At last,
the ground hinged its jaws
to size me up for your feast.
My face tasted floor,
no more than a morsel
spat from blackness,
mauled to exhaustion.

2.

Mummy's roar comes
forceful and foreign.
She takes us to a tamer
famed for caging tigers
in rooms with strange clocks.

He says:
The trick to survive
is to try and describe
how *it arrived* –
when teatimes turned tables into fables.

Time shifts its hands in our laps,
paws at my throat,
your tail a pendulum
ticking forbidding.

I ache to stop –
just hold my tongue
'til you dissolve me.

But Mummy is right to worry;
my body
a house gulped hollow,
ghost-riddled home,
poem of bones.

3.

So I spill the tale of The Tigress
Poached In The Night:

my spasm-grabbed mother,
her body a hand I held with my heart,
her face a prayer in my palms.

In spite of shaking,
came her brave smile – a straight line
that drew my pledge
to care for her cub,
my cuddle of brother,
safe in his feather den,
stalking dreams.

He didn't hear the doorbell
that swallowed her whole:
honed medical tones,
jungle of footsteps,
pounce of headlights.
All these knives
found our dead night.

I watched long after she'd gone – wide open –
the promise scooped tight to my chest,
letting this
striped arrival
bite at my lips.

The Girl with Feet for Teeth

Okay, her parents say.
That's enough.
Time to get it looked at.

In the waiting room
she grinds her feet.
No-one can tell if the sound

is a kick or a scream.
She runs on empty,
teeth heavy, words

sucked-in like a belly.
They call her name.
She isn't ready.

The white-coat asks her
how on earth she eats
with feet for teeth –

the perfect question
for a perfect *freak.*
Her parents tell him lies

of tiptoe bites, pickpocket light.
Her voice, a calcium callous,
cracks.

They made her swap
her feet for teeth.

No more running scared –
now she smiles back

and sinks her plaque
into tougher crusts,

showing the past how it feels
to eat her dust.

11 Weeks Since the Accident

with thanks to Lisa

Little one looks up and beams. *Nanny, you're normal again?* she asks. The job is to nod and hug. Outside, in the car, she sobs the question up. Each week is a different episode of past that hinges on a door slammed wide. She used

to have a weightless smile – an easy call and quick response. Now, she waits for normal days when smiles no longer feel like fakes or wilfulness rejecting fate or memories returning shapes.

A Climb Too Far

with thanks to Paul

/

By dusk, the boys were spent.
The river's glimpse of tomorrow
shot ahead. Three of them

swam for help.
Behind them,
the canyon
flooded fast.

They ripped
themselves free
of the water
and panicked
through brambles,
numb to the thorns
tearing their legs.

\\

At dawn,
a search party
followed the river –
quick as a fist –
and tried not to think
of them dead.

Up there!
Alive by the whim of a ledge.

Relief was the sweetness
of blackberries,
hot as the moral
of blood.

///

Now, as men, the smile that tears between them
carries their flood: a bit like shame, a lot like trust.

Meeting an Acquaintance on an Anxious Day

I will open stiffly, like a tricky jar: *Hello.* You'll stop, acknowledge, *Oh – hi!* and look
at me, expectant, waiting for my jam. I'll touch your eyes with mine – brief as a pinch –

and let go, stung by your flinch. I'll ask if you're okay these days. *Not bad,* you'll say, *Not bad.*
Not good? I'll ask – and give you leave to moan – language of hands, gesture of tone.

Our pause will feather past, nervous of next. The stems beside your eyes will barely sway
when the bird lands. You'll take me up on my cue to talk about your boss and the family.

I'll try to tune you in, clear my static box and jolt the fuzz away. But as you speak, I'll notice
your truant whisper of hair, screaming straight up against the light – and I'll want to tell you

about it. I'll want to reach out and pat it down. The shock of this urge will dislodge a smile, which I'll skilfully purge. Now, I'll think about my edges – check my lips for spills, suddenly

hate how I'm standing and shift. *Other than that I'm great,* you'll say, *how about you – are you okay?* You'll hand me the question, wrapped like a gift, *a thank you for caring a bit.* Guilty,

I'll give you the answer we deserve: *I'm fine,* I'll lie. The perfect swerve. You'll pop it in a pocket, look past me for a beat. I'll ghost into fragments gratefully. Time for our last sweet

words – we'll spoon them from the jar: *Good to see you... Yeah, let's make sure to meet.*

We'll close our lids and split the
street between us: a gobbled treat.

In Formation

We hang here,
swallows treading air,
in case the photo didn't take.

A thumbs-up
from the eager hunter
lets our wings retract

from disembodied backs.
Our features figure out their codes.
We guess, as if we've never known

the way we act
when we're relaxed.
Some fly towards the camera

for the evidence. We don't.
We are the ones who flinch
or blink, so unprepared for this.

In years to come, I hope
you'll hold this photo up
and note how much has changed,

but please don't assume
from this face alone
how [add emotion here] I felt today.

How many reasons do you have to smile?

With thanks to Xeno

An ice-cream
in the sun is one.
   The drip
     from here
     to now
     to gone.

Do you smile
with your eyes
open or closed?

Experiment – try it both ways.
Press your lips together.
Stretch your cheeks.

At first, it's fake, a Mona Lisa,
panning for gold
in a foolish crowd,

until a scoop of serotonin
sends its ghostly flavour
through your mouth.

Next, there are
three brief stages
(any order counts):

one) you break a part &
two) you cast a spell &
three) you melt deliciously
                from gone
                to here
                to now.

Chickpeas con Chorizo for Thanksgiving

With thanks to Anita and her Abuela Pilar

It's been two hours already
and still, she is stirring the pot
in her English kitchen.

Minutes 'til the family descends.

Her arm complains and she is eight again,
perched on a stool, moaning to Abuela.

You'll never get a husband
if you can't stir a pot
for more than two minutes, little girl.

A noisy burst of her descendents
are about to eat those words.

Look at me now Abuela – look!
Here she is, two hours in,
minding the supper,
just like Grandma taught her.

Every turn disturbs the spice of grief.

She circles round herself.
The pride starts deep.
It muscles through her memories,
to spoon an ache between her cheeks.

The herbs she stirs up
twirl around the pot
to surface every time anew.

This is your family, Abuela.
They love your recipe.
They would have loved you too.

At the Birthday Party

Beside the jugs of orange squash
and plates of custard creams,

a boy is telling his friend
about his baby cousin
who loves to sleep.

That's her favourite thing, he says.
She sleeps all day. And when she sleeps,
she smiles. Smiling is her second favourite thing.

His friend is really listening.

One day, she slept forever, the boy explains,
his voice the imprint in a morning pillow.
That's how much she loves to sleep. She never stops!

She smiles like this, he says – and shows it off.

It sings through his whole body:
a tuning fork for lullabies,
the light his sadness has become.

His friend picks up the jug of squash
and, smiling, pours them both a cup.

Sketch

With thanks to Emily

A lined-paper day.
Commuter time.
The Northern line.
The tube is not

completely packed
but cramped enough
that every seat is filled
with someone buttoned up.

As usual, the strangers,
close enough to touch,
avoid each other's eyes,
their lowered shutters stuck.

A lady hears a pencil scratch.
Up, up and away – she flutters
from her book, to see the artist
opposite return her look.

He draws some more,
then holds the paper up,
to show a simple smiley face
in simple graphite grey.

A paperweight inside her lifts.
All the eyes around them notice too
and pass their souls around a bit.
It's brief, but everyone is cheerful

in this living sketch,
so when the world resumes
its hurried scrawl, they feel
a little more prepared.

Crying in Front of the TV

You haven't noticed yet
and anyway, I'm not crying.

It's the television weeping pixels.
I am just a mirror full of blur,

a box of light and wires
switched to a certain frequency.

I'm a full-body throat
swallowing myself in silence.

You turn to make a joke or tell me
some nerdy trivia about the film.

I don't dare look at you
in case it trips my fuse,

but the angle
of my jaw gives me away. Suddenly,

we're smiling – a half-frame flash
as we notice my emotion, which is natural.

We pull each other closer,
tune into the same channel,

let the shared electric
of our moment settle.

Service with a Smile

with thanks to Saili

Over by the glasses frames
and oddly tiny mirrors,
he spots the lady in the raincoat
being difficult.

A colleague throws that look
of amber on the brink of red, so
he's beside them in an instant.
Always an *urgent* task to invent.

His colleague escapes
and the lady turns her smile on him –
a smile that's heard
it's always right.

Here, in this shop, she is brave,
a spectacle of pent-up shakes.
Rewound, like a neck, through
the doors, she wouldn't be so sure.

He hands her a look of compassion
like a pack of tissues.
It's the final straw – all it takes
to turn her tear-ducts raw.

She's conscious of the strangers,
so he guides her
to the corner with the sofas.
It's been difficult, she sobs

and gestures to the rack of frames.
I don't have savings for a rainy day.
She meets his eyes, ashamed,
anticipating rows of small-print.

Instead, he shows her loopholes;
discounts she can clamber through.
His face is an honesty box, a sign
that reads: *this smile is not for sale.*

She leaves with a pair of glasses
that suit her for the first time in her life,
feeling right for the first time
and not just by right.

The Startling Impact of Shoes

with thanks to Jodie

An older man waits for his lift,
a pair of spitfires trailing him.

He swivels on his stick.
You sound like a fighter-pilot from the Blitz!

The stranger stops, absorbs and peals,
her safety-lock unthrottled as the chocks release.

She's 5ft 2 with a power-walk to match.
They sit together for a while and chat.

His stories have a sorrow, light with flight.
They rest a precious layer on the runways of his eyes.

Soon – *I can't believe the time!* – she has to go.
She leaves him waiting for his lift.

He thinks he's made her day;
she thinks she's brightened his.

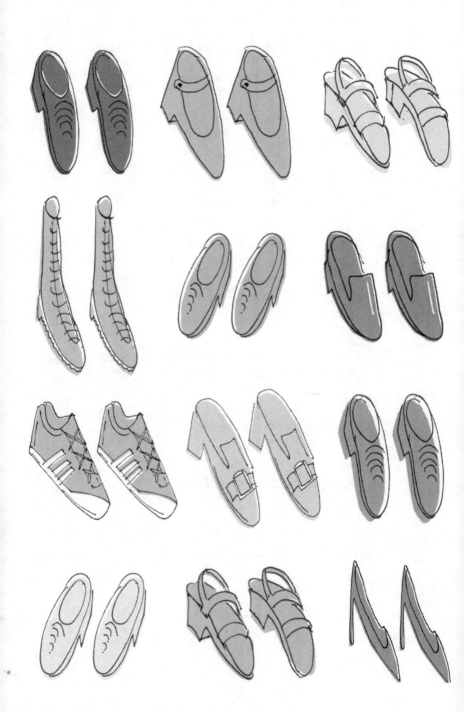

Keep Searching

with thanks to Debra

Happiness is the time that magazine chose you and him,
out of all the couples at the party, to represent the face of fun.

Your smiles that night were a double-page spread. Timeless
as heartache. Your gloss was anything but fake. Beside you,

the man who knew how good he had it. The photographer's card
has gone. One day, you'll find it and send for a copy.

Joy will halve itself open in your hands,
and oh! – the thrill of it – you'll notice only yours.

A Distant Signal Flickers

You're a stranger, waving at me
from across the street
and I am acknowledged,

finally seen.
Someone I don't yet recognise
salutes my aloneness.

Beaming, I raise my hand
and surrender myself like a flag.
We are two light-houses

linked across the flood.
The others come and go –
they barely notice – to and fro.

Waving, we are linked, the same.
I see your smile   glitch   like a flame,
the frozen screen of a blank face.

You tilt a little to the side
and cast your beam towards a distant ship.
I'm caught in the middle,

a spanner in the works,
a pantomime fool
with the worst behind me.

Our circuitry is broken
but I flicker nonetheless.
I thought you had reached out

across all that vastness to wave at me,
a small acknowledgement.
At least I know,

logistically, it's possible.

S i mile

A simile is
like two strangers exchanging
an unlikely smile

or two friends on a
sleep-over, swapping secrets
between separate beds.

After School

for Rosie

Village

It's our stop
at the top of the hill.

I hold your bag
while you get your bike.

You'll push it all the way
to walk with me, despite the rain.

We drift up Water St
like careless pooh-sticks,

bouncing gossip,
sparking arguments.

At times, I catch the scent
of laundry – familiar as mine.

We reach the crossroads,
where we hold goodbye

between us like a kite.
I tease left, you right.

We linger here for minutes –
just one last thing

and one last *thing*
and one *last* thing,

until we scrap goodbye
and fall in step together,

bound for yours – a plan in
motion, hatched unspoken.

Over the gate, we plunder
the greenhouse for goodies:

plump-fuzzy suns
you test with your thumb

and pass me to taste
and the taste is love,

like the first time you said hello
to my lonely book

and your voice
was apricot.

Into your porch, shoes kicked off,
we squeeze our knees by the fire.

Your mum brings us milk,
warm and thick,

the flavour of cud,
a three-course meal to glug.

City

That was then and this is now:
a concrete day in a pasteurised town.

I hold my bag while you flag the bus.
This time you don't climb up.

We can't drift back
to milk and apricots.

I want to say
one last thing

and one last *thing*
and one *last* thing

but we don't.

All we do is smile,
that same old toothy goodbye,

the scent of laundry –
familiar as mine.

First Class

with thanks to Ellie

Two students are sitting
in the wrong compartment of the train.

One is staring into sunlight;
streamers on a face.

The other smiles widely;
cheeks begin to ache.

They catch each other's thoughts
as business people tap on silent laptops.

One stowaway begins to shake,
which makes the other giggle too.

Scruffiness in all those suits.
A pack of party rings to share.

All that happiness
without the fare.

A Solo Rescue Mission
to Weston-Super-Mare

I've got too many things to do,
so I've run away to Weston
for a dose of freshness – to clear

my head of silly lists and ticks.
Out there, beyond the pier,
is only the truth.   The sky

a vague remembrance of rain.

And all this sand beneath
my feet – so soft, so forgiving.
Nothing to do but breathe.

Falling Over at the Festival

Mud, I love the way you squirt.
Why is your name dirt?

Give me your cosy squelch, your throaty belch,
your global system, sucking a thousand soles.

Give me your puddlish pulse and carcass grass.
(Ignore the strangers trying not to laugh.)

I want to fall over
all over again,
scramble home to you, haggle hope
from your slimy banks.

Beautiful mud!
Let caked, excalibur hands return my thanks.
Let me get down to earth,
grant me gravity's
cold dead weight
and gross rebirth.

I want to throw huge pies of your soul.
I want to crawl around in your clay and turf.

What are you, mud?
Are you earth's blood?
Are all these pulsing worms your veins?
Are you some ancient modern art piece?
Do you condone play-dough?

Festival friend, festival foe.
Hellish alter-ego of snow.

I feel you beneath my feet,
in my hair, in my mouth,
impossibly tucked between my toes.

I feel you, soft, solemn and slow;
your faint sub-surface flow,
ebb, suck and swallow.

I'm sorry to pile you with questions, mud.
You fascinate me – you leave me for dust.

I have spilled my cider thanks to you
but I'm having far too much fun
to care what anyone thinks –

and this slide to freedom
is worth the loss of a drink.

Face-Planting

In the kitchen
with its window – a sheet
of unmade sky,
she slumps in her pot,
limp, dramatic, all joy lost
to the anxious night.

Go on, move: pour her a glass
from the tap, wet her throat,
and turn to drink one too.

The earth – a hot,
compacted headache –
breaks its grip.

Look round – *Wow!*
That was quick!
She's up, dressed, ready to live.
All her loving fingers reach.

Another instant
and my face
is in her body,
my hands on the table,
a prayer of green.

You'll find me like this,
at the end of the world,
bent double into endless leaves,
breathing in peace.

Prototypes

'The Earliest Bird' – Bristol Museum and Art Gallery

In the early days of our love,
we found your exhibit in the museum.
Experts named you The Earliest Bird –
although you didn't really fly.

Your progress was more of a glide,
the slightest stone thrown through time,
but they saw potential on your sleeves;
the ancient part of you had prototypes to preen

with something like a beak
and quick, reptilian teeth.
We're in our kitchen
on a winter morning.

Outside, the world is feathered with frost.
Since move-in day, we've longed for birds.
Today, after months of leaving out seeds
like bribes for thieves, your distant relative

ventures in – a scrappy robin,
primed to feast. We watch through
the window, clutched in our rented
nest. Love is the last dinosaur left.

We feel like the first cave-age couple
to witness your draft attempt at flight;
the first two humans to hold
each other quite this tight.

In years to come, perhaps some other beasts
will find *our* bones in stone
and wonder why we ever
let this feeling go.

The Politics of Washing Up

A carcass of plates
sways between us.

My words, polished, glint.
I hear yours harden in reply.

This argument is far from clean.
Our best intentions gather grime.

I want to wipe
your careless smile away;

you want to wipe
the righteousness from mine.

The more we smile,
the less polite we feel.

Animals bare our teeth
beside a prize.

You dodge my words
like plates, dazed.

How is this such a crime?
You've helped me so many times.

You fold my criticism
in defensive – no, protective – arms.

Out of nowhere, comes my *sorry*
and my outstretched heart.

We pick the carcass
clean together,

swaying along to our favourite song.
I wash – you dry.

Sexy Recycling

'Ah love, let us be true to one another!' –
Matthew Arnold, Dover Beach

Home from a long shift,
see-through with tiredness,
you sort our recycling in the rain.

You won't let me help,
so I lean in the doorway,
mocking you softly.

You stamp on soggy cardboard,
crush cans in strong hands,
and swear at anything that says

it can't be recycled – yet.
Watching you work, I know
this moment won't degrade.

Tonight will be recycled in my mind
until we're clinging onto life
like polar bears to ice.

We'll drift for decades on a raft of thick debris,
debating what our Desert Island Discs will be
until, at last, we can't resist the sea.

Here, on our wistful street, it's late.
Curtains flinch at the drunken tumble of glass.
A fox propels its sideways tease.

All you want to do right now
is sit down, kick your shoes off
and fold away the day.

Raindrops grope your neck
and soak your shirt to the skin.
My heat is rising faster

than the atmosphere –
that's not the ozone tingling...
forget ripped jeans, tight tops,

and all that rot.
Doing the right thing
is honestly the origin of hot.

On Indecision

When I was 23,
babies were aliens to me.

I feared their hostile scrunch,
their screaming policy
and sleep atrocities.

Then, at 24,
the jealous, deadly horde

of hormones I remember from my teens
developed soft new eyes in me
and babies have occupied my dreams.

Every month, at period time, I hold
my partner's palm to my stomach.

The weight of it, placed on the ache
of my cramp-side, can patiently
siphon the pain from my bank-slide.

Lately, doing this brings
thoughts of alien fists.

This touch-down on my belly's moon
ignites an ET ode to home – we're barely
a phone-call from parenthood.

Invaded by babies, a day-dream too soon,
we clench at the pressure, cradle our youth

and, every month, I shed my womb.
At times, we glimpse the fizz of her
and blow her away like a fuse.

We tie her unpopped balloon to the spacecraft
and count down from ten.

When certain people
ask when I plan to wind my clock
– *you don't have forever you know* –

I laugh,
like an empty purse,

at their fable of family,
tell them nuclear's expensive
and I'm a poet.

Every dream they ever sacrificed
for happiness reminds their faces of fear.

Their buried hopes explode at me
from fission eyes – confusion strikes.
As kids, they learned that hope like mine

meant gambling the concrete of a token life.
The future isn't fixed these days,

so I roll out all the dreams
I haven't gone full-term with,
all the legacies to birth.

I imagine, with horror, my belly full of alien
and name my brooding a nightmare. Escapable.

And then I think of my mum,
our bond a chord so musical
the sound is a new colour to describe.

I think of her birthing my dreams into being,
coaxing her poem to write.

Imagine we never were – never forged –
our spark to molten mud.
At this, I feel sick with decision

all over again,
like a morning, as yet, unbroken.

Life Experience

On the snowy road below
my window, a boy is bundled up
for the arctic expedition
of walking to school.

His siblings dash ahead,
kicking up flocks of snow.
A parent holds him
by a glove.

This is his first true enigma.
You can tell because he sways
as if the ground might sink
at any

second,
a half-formed astronaut,
encumbered by nothing, yet,
but too much love.

He breaks free,
bends down, scoops
a sample up and holds it
to the red stove of his cheek.

The cold is a paper-cut
he stops to wonder at,
his face a simmer of extraordinary,
but wisdom calls him

from the end of the road
and I am almost
(not-quite) ready
to follow them.

Dancing on the Patio

Here, completely still, I dance
beneath the lemon slice of morning.
Pulp forms in billows from afar

but I know it's a fiction of my own citrus.
This is the dance I've learned;
to ride the rind of joy, not peel it off

by telling myself it's almost gone –
the sharp, exposed surprise
I knew was coming all along.

This kind of twist is good.
I've always had a taste for sour things –
they have a kick, a zing, a thrill

that can't be felt at first
but waits to find its final stop.
The kind of joy that thinks a lot.

Behind the double-doors, agape
where I left them, the rest of the day
is squeezed too tight.

Only this moment is wide –
just me, the sky,
and a slab of land.

I cup the world
like a fruit
in my hands.

Baby Steps

I'm told she never crawled;
just sat, like a sack of potatoes, for ages,
while fellow babies
raced the corners

of the nursery –
clumsy compasses
exploring their four points
for the first time.

I wonder
if she ever thought
she'd never walk.
From what I know now,

I'd guess her gummy brain
began to mouth at doubt,
but of course, I can't be sure.
It's too far back.

One day
she walked – just like that! –
seized the ceiling of her latitude,
pulled her milky body up,

chin to fist,
and felt her fingernail steps
cut their quicks.
So now, when doubt

stops me standing up,
I try to summon that other me,
of sterner stuff,
who never tried to crawl,

but waited to be brave enough
to risk the fall.

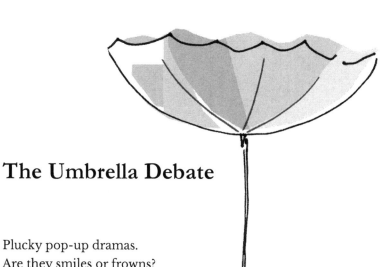

The Umbrella Debate

Plucky pop-up dramas.
Are they smiles or frowns?
They keep the rain away,

but, if they're smiles,
they're upside-down.
Beneath their charm,

our fallacies feel less pathetic,
though they don't
hold up to any force.

Light on muscle,
they tend to buckle
under heavy storms.

I almost wish I didn't have
this in-built faulty parasol
that leaps at every hint of grey.

Maybe then, you
wouldn't look at me
and think I'm weather-proof

against your rain.

Clifftops

1.

We have arrived.
Heartbeats woken by the climb. Coastline in your smile.

Below,
the sleep of shingle, fishermen's patience,
waves dreaming of dancing.

You say *I'll show you how it's done,*
                                        kiss me
                                        and jump.

2.

All of a sudden, I have been here before.
Live anxiety climbs my spine –
its deft feet dig waves from a distant brain.

Last time I came to Swanage
was a trip to the coast with school,
a clatter of classmates
freed for the week
from lesson plans
and second hands.

It rushes back to me, cold as the slap of sea;
hands damp with panic,
breath wet with attack,
cliff-faced crumbling.

See their easy outlines:
girls in H&M and giggles;
boys outgrown by their noses.
To me, they were gods –
grins full of evil.

Safe on my clifftop,
I feared them from afar,
their shallow-splash flirting.
Fingers' graffiti on sand carved
We were here, 2005.
Teenage legacies, soon to be ironed by tide.

I kept my watch,
a lone rock-pool left by their oceans,
snug in my niche: the shy girl who liked to read.

Back then,
life was the chink of light under the door;
the book-down come-downs
in grey dawns, wondering
when did I shrink to the margins of my own story?

Mine was a world of magic trees, rings, ships and ink,
warm and dry within the lines of print.

School was fruit instead of ice-cream.
Other kids were strawberries – all their pips on show.
I was a lemon: wax and rind outside
so unkind words slid off me at the time
but when I squeezed their meaning
out of me, the taste was citrus.

I shed my sugar
for the pulp of their pride
and slowly lost my zest for life.

This mouth turned uncertain.
Terror tripped on my tongue –
tongue-tides in clumsy courtship of the shore.

Instead, I clung to a voice inside,
tones I know like the chug of my own blood:
Keep still, my love. Stay away from living.
Others do it better.

3.

Now back to the splash you make
when you break your fall with my heart
and come up smiling.

Hours have slept since then. Your hair is barely wet.
The moon's a post-it note from hope.

I feel you feel me breathe again. Lips stretch their coastline.
The mocking black,
my sobbed intent,
your confidence.
I push my past off the ledge
                    and
                    leap
                    in pursuit.

        Body shocks with sense,
        claws for warmth, reaches for rock,
up and out to your arms' calm pond.

Below,
breakers applaud,
fishermen burst,
my soul floods horizons.

This is my clifftop:
anxiety, lonely as heaven –

but I will not die like a wave,
dreaming of dancing.

THANKYOUS

A great big ridiculous grateful grin to everyone who has helped
me to find my smile, especially those who have been there when
the umbrella turned inside out.

Extra special thanks to:

Sally, Mark and Joe Calverley, plus my grandparents, my entire
family and my friends for their love and encouragement.

Chris Beale for being my 'calm pond', enabling me to believe in
myself and proof-reading every poem.

Malaika Kegode, Tom Sastry and Helen Mort for helping me to
see the collection from fresh angles.

Kieran O'Shea for the magical illustrations. Kieran and his
brother Ryan also designed and built The Poetry Machine.

Bethany M. Roberts for helping to develop my voice through
our music and poetry collaboration: House of Figs.

To the varied organisations who have supported my poetry over
the years, including: Above & Beyond, Apples & Snakes, Arts
Council England, Arvon, BBC Radio Bristol, Bristol Tonic, East
Harptree Primary School, Harptrees Arts Festival (especially
Paul), Milk Poetry, Mr B's, Raise The Bar, Storysmith Books,
The Prince's Trust, University Hospitals Bristol NHS
Foundation Trust (especially Anna) and the University of Leeds
(especially Tess).

Anyone who has taken part in The Poetry Machine, been to
one of my group sessions, watched one of my performances or
cheered me on from afar: you are the reason this book exists...

Last but not least, a big beaming thank you to Stuart
Bartholomew and Verve Poetry Press for being the kindest,
most supportive home for these smile poems.

ABOUT VERVE POETRY PRESS

Verve Poetry Press is a quite new and already award-winning press that focussed initially on meeting a local need in Birmingham - a need for the vibrant poetry scene here in Brum to find a way to present itself to the poetry world via publication. Co-founded by Stuart Bartholomew and Amerah Saleh, it now publishes poets from all corners of the UK - poets that speak to the city's varied and energetic qualities and will contribute to its many poetic stories.

Added to this is a colourful pamphlet series, many featuring poets who have performed at our sister festival - and a poetry show series which captures the magic of longer poetry performance pieces by festival alumni such as Polarbear, Matt Abbott and Geraldine Carver.

In 2019 the press was voted Most Innovative Publisher at the Saboteur Awards, and won the Publisher's Award for Poetry Pamphlets at the Michael Marks Awards.

Like the festival, we strive to think about poetry in inclusive ways and embrace the multiplicity of approaches towards this glorious art.

www.vervepoetrypress.com
@VervePoetryPres
mail@vervepoetrypress.com